SAN FRANCISCO

SAN FRANCISCO

Introduction by
Bill Pronzini

Photography by
Larry Lee
Mark Stephenson
and
West Light

Produced by Boulton Publishing Services, Inc., Toronto
Designed by Fortunato Aglialoro

©1985 Oxford University Press (Canadian Branch)
SKYLINE PRESS is a registered imprint of the Oxford University Press

ISBN 0-19-540626-5
1 2 3 4 – 8 7 6 5
Printed in Hong Kong by Scanner Art Services, Inc., Toronto

SAN FRANCISCO IS JUST SAN FRANCISCO, AND THAT'S ALL THERE IS TO IT

an Introduction by Bill Pronzini

San Francisco is like Venice and Athens in having strange memories; she is unlike them in being lit from within by a large and luminous hope. Wonder and terror may pass over her spirit; still nothing changes her purpose, nothing weakens her courage.

IRA G. HOITT

San Francisco — no well-bred American, unless he comes from Chicago, ever says 'Frisco' — is a delicious combination of wealth and wickedness, splendour, and squalor, vice, virtue, villainy, beauty, ugliness, solitude and silence, rush and row — in short San Francisco is just San Francisco, and that's all there is to it, as they say there.

GEORGE GRIFFITH

San Francisco is many things to many different people, natives and visitors alike.

For some, it is a city of magnificent vistas. The downtown skyline, the bright blue Bay and its spanning bridges, the long chain of East Bay communities as seen from high atop Twin Peaks . . . the entrance to the Golden Gate, glimpsed through the woods of Lincoln Park and Land's End . . . the graceful curve of Ocean Beach, the vast sweep of the Pacific broken only by bird-limed Seal Rock and the distant Farallone Islands, as viewed from the Cliff House or Sutro Heights . . . the cityscape, and Alcatraz and Angel islands, as seen from the Marin County side of the Golden Gate Bridge . . . these, and dozens more, from a panoramic kaleidoscope that, once witnessed, can never be forgotten.

For others, San Francisco is a city of hills — fifty-three of them, to be exact, large and small. Some are surmounted by landmarks: Grace Cathedral and the Mark Hopkins and Fairmont hotels atop Nob Hill; Coit Tower rising from the top of Telegraph Hill; the massive white cross at the crest of Mount Davidson, where Easter Sunday sunrise services are held. San Francisco's most famous landmarks — its cable cars, in use here since 1873 — inch up and thunder down these and others of the fifty-three. The lesser-known elevations are crowned by parks (there are a total of 74 within the city's boundaries), by homes and public buildings, by reservoirs; one (Lone Mountain) is even the site of a small college campus. No one who visits this compact metropolis (46.38 square miles) can fail to be impressed by the number, size, and in some cases frightening steepness of our hills.

For still others, San Francisco is a city of architectural variety and contrasts. The Golden Gate and Bay bridges . . . among its many skyscrapers, the pyramid-shaped Transamerica Building (which one local columnist has described, tongue-in-cheek, as an upside-down ice cream cone) . . . its multitude of churches that range from the old-California Spanish style of Mission Dolores, to the Romanesque Saint Peter and Saint Paul, to the neo-Byzantine Temple Emannu-El, to the Russian ecclesiastical architecture of the Holy Virgin Cathedral of the Church in Exile . . . the French Renaissance design of City Hall and the War Memorial Opera House . . . the ornate Corinthian columns of the Palace of Fine Arts . . . the ancient-pagoda-style facades along Grant Avenue in the heart of Chinatown . . . and of course, the renowned 'painted ladies' — row after row of Queen Anne, Stick, and Italianate Victorians stretching along the hillsides and flatlands of Pacific Heights, the Haight-Ashbury, Potrero Hill, and the Mission District, the greater percentage of them refurbished and repainted in vivid modern colors. You can't travel more than a few blocks anywhere in this city without seeing something different and unusual in the style of its buildings.

And for still others, San Francisco is a fascinating melting pot of ethnic and cultural lifestyles. In few other urban environments will you find the variety of neighborhoods that exist here, in this place Northern Californians refer to simply as 'The City': Chinatown, the thriving miniature *ginza* called Japantown, Italian North Beach, the Russian settlement around outer Geary Boulevard, the Church Street German enclave, the Latino quarter along Mission Street, the new Vietnamese and Cambodian communities that are reclaiming the once-bleak Tenderloin, even the Castro Street and Polk Gulch areas that San Francisco's gay population has made its own. The downtown and neighborhood streets teem with people of every race and color — an ethnic mix that, among other things, provides the variety and quality of The City's world-famous restaurants.

For me, San Francisco is a precious gem comprised of all these facets — and one other, equally as important. For me, this is and always will be a city of mystery.

It is San Francisco, after all, that spawned what is surely the most famous of all American detective stories (and one of the most famous of all American films, thanks to the genius of Humphrey Bogart and John Huston) — Dashiell Hammett's classic tale of Sam Spade, Brigid O'Shaughnessy, and the quest for a marvelous, jewel-encrusted black bird, *The Maltese Falcon*. In this 1929 novel (and in his earlier series of stories featuring the Continental Op), Hammett introduced readers everywhere to the sights and sounds and smells of San Francisco. Introduced them to its cable cars and ferry boats, its Victorian mansions and polite (and not so polite) society, its rebels and oddball characters, its Chinatown intrigues real and imagined; to the sinuous, blanketing fogs, the steep hills, and menacing, little-known alleys, the sinister emptiness of the waterfront at night; and to the speakeasies and gambling dens, the rumrunners and hatchetmen and Tenderloin sharpies. He recreated and fictionalized The City as no one has since, as perhaps no one ever will again. He made it a living, breathing, shadowy, thrilling entity in the imaginations of a generation of literate people.

Hammett knew whereof he wrote, for he lived — and worked as a Pinkerton detective — in San Francisco throughout the Prohibition '20s. Things here have changed a great deal since his time, and yet in another sense they have changed little. Except for the disappearance of the rumrunners and the speakeasies, the essence of Hammett's San Francisco lingers on. The cable cars and Victorian mansions are still here, as are a new breed of ferry boats. The rebels and oddball characters, the hatchetmen and Tenderloin sharpies are still here too. The fogs are no less sinuous and blanketing — foghorns still echo mournfully in the midnight hours — and the byways of Chinatown are no less secret, the little-known alleys no less menacing, the waterfront no less sinister after dark.

To a large extent it is this essence of mystery which, for the past half-century, has inspired writers (myself among them) to use San Francisco as a setting for hundreds of novels and short stories. (The same is true of filmmakers. Think of San Francisco in terms of theatrical cinema, and you think of the *Thin Man* series, *Experiment in Terror, Bullitt, Dirty Harry, Foul Play,* and of course *The Maltese Falcon*. Think of it in terms of radio and television shows and you think of *The Adventures of Sam Spade, The Fat Man,*

Lineup, Ironside, The Streets of San Francisco, Partners in Crime.) Unlike Southern California, which a number of its resident writers consider a state of mind, San Francisco is a self-contained *presence.* If I may say this without sounding provincial, and with all due respect to my friends and neighbors to the south, one can write about Los Angeles with a certain detached, analytical objectivity, as such luminaries as Raymond Chandler and Ross Macdonald have done so beautifully. Writing about San Francisco — writing about it well — requires a deep subjective involvement.

For this is a visceral city, much as New York and London are on a larger scale; it can rarely be treated, as Southern California often is, as an abstract. It throbs with tight-packed life, it assaults the senses; its flavour is sometimes bitter, sometimes sweet, but always sharp and distinctive. Aside from its obvious visual attractions, one of the things that makes it such a desirable setting for fiction and film is that it is a memorable character in its own right — a tough, quirky, uncompromising, cynical, idealistic, happy, sad, callous, big-hearted, vibrant personality, full of conflict and emotion, hiding parts of itself behind its wind-whipped cloak of fog. Sam Spade, the quintessential private eye, could have operated in no other city in the world; he and San Francisco were made for each other, because fundamentally they are one and the same.

Another reason for The City's popularity as a place of fictional drama and melodrama is that things *happen* here. Because of its cosmopolitan nature, its turbulent history, its free-spirited lifestyle, the Bay Area has long been known as a bastion of all types of liberalism. In that sense it is ultra-modern, reflecting vividly and immediately, in microcosm, the changes and upheavals in American society. It is an environment where causes are born and nurtured, where beatniks and flower children and others of the so-called counterculture have flourished and continue to flourish. In San Francisco in the past few decades we have had political and student unrest, political scandal and assassination, riots, radical activism of various types and degrees, social nonconformity, and the gradual establishment of the largest gay community in the world. San Franciscans do not take pride or pleasure in all these things, but each phenomenon in its own way intrigues us, and each in its own way enhances The City's image of uniqueness, of something strange and wonderful.

Baghdad-by-the-Bay (another name by which San Francisco is known) does not stand alone as an allure for writers, film-makers, visitors from all over the globe. Within a hundred and fifty miles of the Golden Gate and Bay bridges are the Mother Lode, rich in California and Gold Rush history; the ancient waterways of the Sacramento River Delta and the deceptively sleepy agricultural towns and villages of the San Joaquin Valley; the splendor of Lake Tahoe and the Sierra Nevada wilderness; the Napa and Sonoma valleys, where some of the world's finest wines are produced; the towering redwoods and giant Sequoias of the North Coast; the rugged Pacific coastline, along which genuine bootleggers plied their trade during Hammett's time; the South Coast fishermen's town of Monterey, home of Steinbeck's Cannery Row, and its neighbors, Carmel and Big Sur.

There is something for everyone here, you see. Vistas, hills, diverse architecture, ethnic potpourri, a tradition and aura of mystery, a wide range of surrounding attractions — and more, so much more. The superb photographs in this book capture some of San Francisco's flavor and beauty, as much as can possibly be captured by a camera; for this city, this presence, must be experienced to be fully appreciated. Those of us who live here know that; those of you who have visited us know it too.

Those of you who have never been to San Francisco . . . why don't you make plans to come? Ours is a friendly city, too, despite its eerie fogs and its other mysteries.

And once you've been here for a few days, you'll understand perfectly what we mean when we say, 'San Francisco is just San Francisco, and that's all there is to it.'

BILL PRONZINI
San Francisco

1 *(right)* The Golden Gate Bridge over the mile-wide Bay from Fort Point to Marin County was opened in 1937, a steel suspension with a central span of 4,200 feet (see also plates 58–60).

LARRY IFF

2 *(left)* Anna Hyatt Huntington's statue of El Cid greets visitors to the Palace of the Legion of Honor, Lincoln Park.

3 San Francisco wharves and harbor.

MARK STEPHENSON

4 *(left)* The Mission San Francisco de Asís, founded in 1776 and popularly known as Mission Dolores because the original log chapel was sited alongside a stream named for Our Lady of Sorrows. The present adobe church was built in 1782–91 and the basilica to the north in 1916. The chapel gives its name to the Mission District of The City.

5 The Transamerica Pyramid, headquarters of the immense holding company Transamerica Corp., formed by A.P. Giannini in 1928. The 48-storey pyramid was designed by William Pereira and built in 1972 on the site of the old Montgomery block.

6 *(left)* The Victorian Conservatory given by James Lick and Charles Crocker for Golden Gate Park, the largest artificially-made park in the world, a landscape of over 1,000 acres created from unpromising sand-dunes to include miles of lawns, gardens, lakes, waterfalls, and many amenities, several of which are featured later in this book.

7 California Palace of the Legion of Honor (1924), Land's End, with one of the most beautiful settings for a museum in America, known for its fine collection of French paintings and sculpture, and merged (1972) with the de Young and Asian Museums to become the Fine Arts Museums of San Francisco.

8 Seasoned veterans of the streets, Yellow Cab and cable-car, downtown.

9 Kearny Street, late afternoon, named after General Stephen Watts Kearny, a hero of the Mexican war of 1846–48 that is sometimes known as 'the Conquest of California'.

MARK STEPHENSON

LARRY LEE

10 *(left)* and 11 The well-loved cable-cars of San Francisco were invented in the 1870s as a unique way to get up and down The City's impossibly steep hills. The car operates by clutching and releasing an endless motorized cable that runs below the tracks. After 108 years of service the system was suspended for two years from 1982–84, in order that a $59 million renovation program could be carried out. The cars are now running smoothly again, to the delight of residents and visitors alike.

12 *(left)* Sailboats and skyline with the Transamerica building.

13 Paddle-steamer *Eppleton Hall,* with the Coit Tower in the background. The Coit Tower is one of San Francisco's most popular landmarks (see plate 53).

14 Entrance to the Fairmont Hotel, Nob Hill. First called California Street Hill, the Hill became known as Nob Hill after the immensely wealthy men who built themselves palatial homes there once the cable-car had made the Hill accessible to the lower town. Among them were James G. Fair and Mark Hopkins, whose names are recalled by the hotels built on the sites of their mansions.

15 The Mark Hopkins Hotel, Nob Hill; a San Francisco landmark and tradition. Just as the Fairmont can boast one of the finest lobbies in the United States, so the Mark Hopkins has an unsurpassed 'room with a view' in the Top of the Mark.

16 *(left)* Turkish Smoking Room in the Whittier Mansion (1896), Jackson Street, home of the California Historical Society. The society was founded in 1871, reorganized in 1886 and 1922 and is dedicated to the furtherance of California history through publications and discussions. The San Francisco headquarters include a library and an art gallery.

17 Inside the Rotunda, City Hall.

18 Chinatown, a game of chess.

LARRY LEE

19 *(right)* The Chinese district in San Francisco is said to be the largest settlement of its kind outside Asia, fascinating to tourists for its Chinese character of architecture, language (mostly Cantonese), newspapers, markets, pharmacies, theatres, restaurants, dress and daily pursuits.

LARRY LEE

20 *(left)* One of the daily papers, Chinatown.

21 Tai-chi, St Mary's Square. The statue, made of rose granite and stainless steel by Beniamino Bufano, is that of Sun Yat-sen (1866–1925), first president of the Chinese Republic, who twice lived in exile in San Francisco during his time of political struggle.

MARK STEPHENSON

22 *(left)* Succulent Peking ducks are one of the many delights that Chinatown offers to residents and to visitors from all over the world.

23 A Chinese dragon guards the stairway of a department store.

MARK STEPHENSON

24 Vats in Fritz Maytag's Anchor Brewery, home of the famous 'Anchor Steam' beer.

25 *(right)* Lombard Street at dusk.

LARRY LEE

MARK STEPHENSON

26 *(left)* 1,500 people took part in the annual 'Bay to Breakers' run in 1984.

27 Fire-escapes and fresh paint, a sparkling pattern of Pacific light and shadow.

CRAIG AURNESS

28 *(left)* One of the many murals that enliven San Francisco.

29 Flowers for sale, Union Square.

30 *(left)* Windmill, Golden Gate Park.

31 The Haas-Lilienthal House (1886), Franklin Street, in the 'Queen Anne' style, survived the earthquake and fire of 1906 to remain an example of the stately houses of a century ago, and is now the only fully furnished house of its time open to the public, and the home of the Foundation for San Francisco's Architectural Heritage.

32 Victorian architecture on Steiner Street, with the Transamerica building in the background.

33 *(right)* Victorian mansions at Franklin and California Streets.

34 *(left)* Sunset and cloud over the Bay.

35 The Golden Gate at sunset; the name long precedes the bridge. John Charles Frémont, a victor in the Mexican War and a hero of early California, gave this name to the harbor-mouth of San Francisco Bay for the same reason that the ancient Greeks called the harbor of Constantinople 'The Golden Horn',—'the form of the entrance to the bay and its advantages for commerce' (Frémont, 1848).

36 A game of golf at the Lincoln Park course, above the Golden Gate.

37 *(right)* Spring blossoms in Golden Gate Park.

LARRY LEE

38 Port of San Francisco Ferry Building.

39 *(right)* Night falls on Telegraph Hill and Columbus Avenue, and Coit Tower and the Church of Saint Peter and Saint Paul.

40 Bank of California Building.

41 Cable-car at day's end.

42 Ferry Building with the Oakland Bay Bridge beyond.

43 *(right)* Palace of Arts and Science, originally the Palace of Fine Arts, built in 1915 for the Panama-Pacific International Exposition. The only building of the exhibition remaining on site, it has a magnificent dome and colonnade (see plate 64).

MARK STEPHENSON

44 The new St Mary's Catholic Cathedral, built in 1971 after the previous building was destroyed by fire in 1960; famous for the dramatic intensity of its geometric architecture.

45 Pleasure-boats at their moorings, San Francisco Yacht Harbor.

MARK STEPHENSON

46 *(left)* On weekends the Bay comes alive with sailing-boats.

47 Island of Alcatraz (Spanish for 'pelican'); location of the first lighthouse on the Pacific Coast (1854) but known to the world as 'The Rock', site of the famous high-security federal prison 1936–63; now part of the Golden Gate Recreational Area and a popular tour destination.

48 Military graveyard in the Presidio (1776); there were four such small garrison forts built by the Spanish to guard their ports at San Diego, Monterey, San Francisco and Santa Barbara respectively.

49 Fort Point National Historic Site; this northernmost promontory at the south base of the Golden Gate was fortified as long ago as 1776, when the Spaniards selected the Point to guard the Bay. In 1857 the US army modelled Fort Point (1853–61) on Fort Sumter, N.C.; it was three-tiered, with a large courtyard, 149 guns and a garrison of 600 men. The Fort was awarded historic status in 1970, was restored by the National Park Service and is now open to the public.

LARRY LEE

50 Steinhart Aquarium, one of the world's largest collections of marine life, California Academy of Sciences, Golden Gate Park.

51 Morrison Planetarium, California Academy of Sciences, Golden Gate Park.

LARRY LEE

CHARLES O'REAR

LARRY LEE

52 War Memorial Opera House (1932), home of the San Francisco Opera which was formed in 1919 by Gaetano Merola. San Francisco's Opera was the first municipal company in the US to have its own opera house.

53 *(right)* Coit Tower, a 210-feet-tall cylindrical tower built on top of Telegraph Hill in 1933 with a bequest from Lillie Hitchcock Coit (herself an honorary firefighter) to commemorate San Francisco's volunteer firemen. The interior is decorated with murals. The magnificent views make Coit Tower one of the city's major tourist attractions.

54 *(left)* Lombard Street, 'the crookedest street in the world', a kind of driving experience that may well be unique to San Francisco.

55 Japanese Tea Garden (1894), Golden Gate Park.

56 The historic square-rigged *Balclutha*, Pier 43, one of several such antique vessels moored on the north waterfront that, together with the Maritime Museum Building (1939) in nearby Aquatic Park, comprise the National Maritime Museum.

57 *(right)* Fisherman's Wharf, with the sign of Alioto's Fish Company.

58 Surfers under the Golden Gate Bridge; clearance for ships is 222 feet up from the water.

59 *(right)* Looking down on the Golden Gate Bridge; at 746-feet high the bridge-towers were the largest ever built.

GEORGE HALL

CRAIG AURNESS

60 - 61   Golden Gate Bridge in fog, caused when the cold California Current sweeps south from Alaska to collide with the warm inland air coming out from the Central Valley.

62 Cycling in Golden Gate Park.

63 Fog in the hills; above the fog-line the hours of sunshine are one-third more than are registered at sea-level.

64 Palace of Arts and Science (see plate 43) with a morning swan.

65 *(right)* Ocean Beach seawalls at sunset.

CRAIG AURNESS

MARK STEPHENSON

66 *(left)* Looking from Lincoln Park Golf Course towards the Golden Gate Bridge.

67 Horseback-riding on San Francisco's Ocean Beach.

LARRY LEE

68 *(left)* Redevelopment of the Golden Gateway downtown core, with the Transamerica Building, the World Trade Center, the dramatic skyscrapers of the Embarcadero Center and the surrounding towers of the Financial District, completely changed The City's skyline and added a new dimension to its character in the 1960s and '70s.

69 San Francisco is connected by frequent daily ferry-service to Sausalito, Larkspur, Tiburon and Angel Island State Park.

70 Five stories of office and department-store space at the Neiman-Marcus building (1982) are topped by the magnificent stained-glass roof retained from the old City of Paris house.

71 *(right)* The Galleria, Crocker Center, one of San Francisco's newest shopping arcades, named after the Crocker Family, descendants of Charles Crocker, one of the 'Big Four', the men who built the Central Pacific Railroad.

MARK STEPHENSON

72 Balloons shower down on the musicians of the San Francisco Symphony after their opening performance of the season in the superb 3,000-seat Louis M. Davies Symphony Hall (1980).

73 Elegant gowns and tuxedos mark the opening of the Symphony season.

74 Roman Catholic Church of Saint Peter and Saint Paul (1924), Washington Square.

75 Grace Cathedral (1900), Nob Hill, on the former site of the Crocker mansion, whose family gave the land for this, the seat of the Episcopalian Bishopric of California. One of the finest Gothic churches in America, Grace Cathedral is enhanced by a great nave, glorious stained glass, and doors cast from Ghiberti's bronze doors of the Baptistry in Florence, Italy (see also plate 77).

LARRY LEE

76 *(left)* The beautiful and historic Synagogue Congregation Emmanu-El.

77 Organ and stained glass, Grace Cathedral.

CRAIG AURNESS

78 *(left)* Night falls on St Ignatius Heights, the cityscape dominated by the towers of St Ignatius College (1914), and the University of San Francisco (founded by the Jesuit Order as St Ignatius College, 1855).

79 Cable-Car, Powell & Market to Beach & Hyde.

80 Downtown at night with the Bay Bridge.

81 *(right)* Financial District with the Transamerica Building, seen from the Coit Tower.

MARK STEPHENSON

82 *(left)* The San Francisco-Oakland Bay Bridge (1933–36), that crosses from Rincon Hill south of Market Street to the Toll Plaza in Oakland, is the longest steel bridge in the world, with a total extent of 8¼ miles.

83 Neon fisherman, Fisherman's Wharf.

CRAIG AURNESS

84 Ghirardelli Square at the foot of Russian Hill is an outstanding example of preservation and new creation—formerly the site of disused factories, now a brilliant ensemble of fashion, restaurants, galleries and entertainment.

85 *(right)* San Francisco old and new; the downtown skyline from Steiner Street.

CHARLES O'REAR

86 Sunset at Seal Rock; sea-lions were once so common along the coast that there are in fact seven places called Seal Rock, but this is the visitor's favorite.

87 *(right)* A container-ship sets out across the Pacific.

88 *(overleaf)* Night falls on the Golden Gate.
LARRY LEE